W9-CHS-596

Tickner's
DOGS

Distributed in the United States of
America and Canada by Howell Book
House Inc., 230 Park Avenue, New York,
N.Y. 10169

© John Tickner 1988

ISBN 0–87605–950–7

Printed and bound in Great Britain at
The Bath Press, Avon

TICKNER'S
DOGS

Written and Illustrated by
JOHN TICKNER

HOWELL
BOOK HOUSE INC.

FOREWORD

Many years ago, probably during the Neolithic age, some sort of early wolf decided to adopt early man and make him his first friend. The idea was doubtless to make life more comfortable for wolves, but it resulted in a partnership which survives today. Few dog-owners realise that the dominating partner is nearly always at the dog-end of the lead.

In return for the comfort of a home, with food and warmth provided, wolves were prepared to do a little work, such as helping with the hunting and guarding the cave from other wolves.

In this way they convinced man that he had domesticated them, but the most intelligent wolves, who had now become known as dogs, realised that by looking pathetic or cuddly, or both, they could live in comfort without having to work at all.

These became pet dogs and just sat or lay about, only moving at times of emergency, such as feeding time. In civilised countries, which means countries where dogs are top dogs, most of them have managed to make themselves pets.

On the other hand, some dogs became professionals because they found they were given even better food than pet dogs. Dogs of the professional classes today are very highly professional indeed. Sporting hounds, gundogs, guard dogs, guide dogs, sheep dogs and police dogs not only do their jobs professionally and efficiently but love to prove to the public how efficient they are by demonstrations, parades, trials and shows, in their spare time.

Having turned into dogs, man's best friends became split up into breeds – this must have occurred without them noticing what was happening. The ancestral wolf would howl with laughter if he could see what peculiar shapes and sizes many of his descendants have become.

Nevertheless, it is as well to remember that even the smallest and most unlikely-looking canine today is really a wolf in dog's clothing.

John Tickner,
Westhide,
Hereford.

EARLY DOG

Nobody can be sure how early wolf insinuated itself into early man's home, but it almost certainly did so by a confidence trick.

It probably left one of its furry cubs about and lurked until a cave child picked it up and took it back to its unsuspecting cave parents.

'Isn't it sweet?' said the child. 'It's lost and we must give it a home.' And that was that. Father wolf followed, pretending he was looking for the cub, Mother and all the other little wolves moved in and the wolf at the door became the dog on the hearth.

Jackals, coyotes and foxes are also close relatives of dogs but they prefer not to discuss the subject.

DOG PERSONS

There is a theory that dogs and the humans with whom they associate tend to resemble each other. This is sometimes true but not generally so.

Often the dog and the human are directly opposite in appearance, although lack of exercise and an aversion to dieting can produce a remarkable similarity to each other as the years go by.

There are dog persons who make a point of looking like their dogs, usually for publicity purposes. Among these are girl models, stage persons and politicians.

Sporting dog persons are the most easily recognised of all. In addition to a sporting style in dress, they can usually be recognised by ear, having a tendency to talk always as if they were addressing a dog across a ten-acre field.

This is especially true of gundog persons. One can hear their voices, not only at shoots but also at gundog trials, social events and even in general conversation in the street, above the voices of mere non-gundog persons.

Some gundog persons not only wear gundoggy type clothes but tend to look like gundogs which, of course, are usually handsome.

There are many dog persons who are unaware that they share their homes with sporting dogs and consequently they cannot be identified as sporting dog persons.

High on the list of sporting dogs who have decided that it is more comfortable to be pet dogs in towns, are Poodles. Originally they were Continental gundogs and some of them still are. The pet versions, usually miniatures, although willing enough to trip along the pavements behind the high heels of fashionably-dressed women, retain the instincts of their ancestors.

The agility and speed with which some of them will retrieve things, like cakes, has astonished many.

Sporting persons who are associated with sporting animals which are still employed in the activities for which they were invented, are not easily recognised when not dressed for the part.

There is one certain way of identifying them. If you pat one of the hounds and say 'nice dog' they will immediately and indignantly reveal themselves.

Of all dog owners the owners of terriers are the most difficult to spot. Indeed, apart from some countrymen who have the sharp-featured alertness of their canine companions, it is impossible to be certain who is likely to have a terrier about the place.

For one thing, terriers are not owned – they do the owning and their selection of owners is wide. Food, warmth and freedom (often surreptitiously obtained) seem to be their priorities.

So beware. Behind the mildest-looking little man or the dearest-looking dear old lady, there may well be lurking terriers. Also remember that humans associated with terriers can be very chatty and have a tendency to bite.

TOWN DOGS

Because a large proportion of humans lives in towns, it follows that a large proportion of the dog population does too. This means that many dogs only go for walks attached to their two-legged companions by leads.

Cunning dogs, which means most of them, soon learn to take their humans the way they want to go. Even the last 'walkies' of the evening, usually supposed to be to post a letter, can be contrived to last longer than intended. This is done by the dog pretending it sees something nasty in the shadows beyond the lamplight and making a dash for it.

Some so-called dog-owners living in towns think it kind to treat the dog as a cat and let it out to roam around the streets at will.

This especially applies to occupiers of small houses without gardens and to flat people. They are likely quite suddenly to be owners of flat dogs, because loose dogs may enjoy being loose but are unlikely to be so for long in modern traffic conditions.

People who let their dogs come and go as they like or, worse, turn them out, should be shut up themselves. No self-respecting dog should have anything to do with them.

It must not be thought that town dogs necessarily have a lonely life. They may get bored dragging their two-legged companions along the streets on a lead, but where enlightened storekeepers have provided a dog park they can be thoroughly sociable.

Dog gossip is probably as witty, spiteful, flirtatious and generally entertaining in the dog park as conversation is inside the shops and supermarkets. Indeed, some dogs must be as sorry as their owners when the chatting has to stop.

The urge to investigate the outside world is strong in all dogs. Like humans, they are interested in what is going on the other side of the fence.

Town dogs, if they are capable of moving at more than an enthusiastic waddle, take every opportunity of breaking out. This is often provided by enthusiastic gardening persons too intent on gardening to realise they are providing the means for their pets to study other people's gardens.

Although pedigree dogs are now immensely popular with all sorts of pet-owners, some of whom don't know for what purpose they were invented, the mongrel remains top dog in many areas, especially in towns.

Because mongrels are a mixture of several breeds, it follows that their ancestry includes canines specifically evolved for sporting purposes. That is why most of them are so instinctively sporting that they will pursue anything that moves, despite any obstacles in their way.

COUNTRY DOG

The average country dog can have the ideal dog's life. The reference is to the ordinary dog who has a country home, not the professional sporting dogs and hounds who live in organised kennels.

The ordinary country dog usually has a fair-sized country garden in which it can roam happily without getting into trouble. Its garden is usually fenced to keep out unwanted wildlife, like rabbits and small children but it can have endless fun chasing squirrels, annoying hedgehogs and seeing cats off the premises.

On no account must a country dog roam off its own territory any more than a town dog should. If it does it may annoy cattle, sheep and farmers.

Spaniels don't bother to look aristocratic and dignified. They are naturally lively and jolly little dogs and if they find that the person they are accompanying on a walk is looking too serious and being too slow, they soon make him lively, if not particularly jolly.

Spaniels rush about the hedges and through bracken and brambles, looking for something to annoy and make fly up or run out.

They are always enthusiastic and anxious to please – themselves as well as you – and will retrieve almost anything or anybody they find lying about. They are excellent all-round dogs and some of them are too round.

Terriers of all kinds know how to get the best out of life.

Although they are willing to go along with humans if they think there will be some fun for them in the expeditions, they are perfectly happy, probably happiest, when entertaining themselves.

Terriers love going down holes and if they can't find one they will soon make one, especially in gardens.

Non-terrier persons tend to think that the only terriers are white with brown or black blotches – what many people call Jack Russells, only most of them are not.

In fact there are many varieties of terriers, a lot of them belonging to ancient breeds, some of them disguised beneath a lot of fur which makes it difficult to tell the biting end from the other. A real terrier will hunt almost anything that moves.

If one doesn't know much about terriers one should be careful. Do not scold or even stroke anything furry with short legs. It will probably bite.

WORKING DOGS

All dogs probably think of themselves as working dogs, even the fat one that may be sleeping at your feet, dreaming that it is chasing rabbits.

Although many dogs do not really work unless they have to do so, there is a group of professional dogs who know they are so good at their work that they give public displays to prove they can be athletic and aggressive and generally human.

High on the professional efficiency list are the police dogs who pad about looking so official that some rough dogs, non-pedigree of course, call out insulting remarks, especially if the police dogs are attached to policemen.

Police dogs are paid to do some things that come naturally. For them it is a job to be sniffed at.

Sheepdogs are among the most hardworking of all working dogs. At one time they all used to work on the farmland and remote hills, ordering sheep about with only the shepherd looking on and expressing his approval or otherwise. Most of them still do but because someone discovered that sheepdog operas could be as popular with television viewers as are human soap operas, many sheepdogs have become telly-stars.

It is said that there are a few viewers, probably non-dog persons who watch football, who claim that counting sheepdogs is as effective as counting sheep. When they look at sheepdog trials, they say, they can do both. Some non-sheepdogs say the same.

Just as most dogs would claim to be working dogs, so would a great many of them consider themselves to be guard dogs.

There are three types of guard dogs; the professional who walks quietly around estates and factories waiting to jump on anyone or anything not meant to be on the premises, the house guard dog who seems to think that not only must it charge the front door when anybody calls but also shout at the telephone whenever it rings and lastly, the dog who considers all it need do is to open one eye and say 'wuff!' and that only during its self-appointed burglar hours.

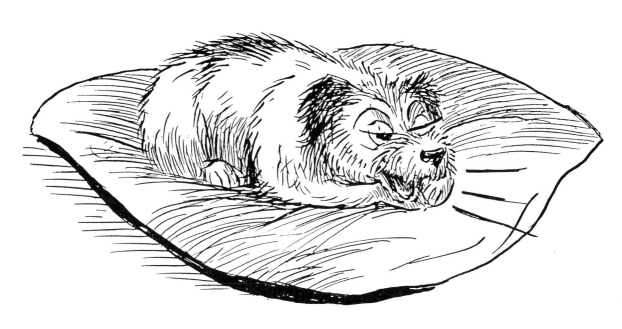

SPORTING DOGS

All dogs are sporting by instinct and many breeds are still employed to be so. Gundogs consider themselves to be superior to other sporting canines, such as hounds, because they perform individually and not in vulgar packs; they are specialists.

Some of the gundog breeds, such as the retriever types, think of themselves as aristocrats and sit about aristocratically on shooting estates, waiting for someone to shoot something.

Even on not so aristocratic shooting estates they manage to look superior while pretending to search for a bird they know is flying serenely onwards. Some are so well-bred that they look the other way when a gun misses something.

In addition to retrievers there are other big gundogs such as Pointers and Setters and several types that have been introduced from Abroad by persons who think we haven't enough of our own.

The duty of Pointers is to point where they think game is lurking, even if their human shooting companion is pointing in the opposite direction. Setters also point where they think game is lurking, only not so vulgarly, and they usually lie down to do it, in a very polite and dignified manner.

The gamekeeper's dog is in the happiest position of all professional dogs. It has the authority of the law combined with the dignity of being the most important dog on a shooting estate.

It follows the keeper about the place, looking important and dignified, sneering at less-important gundogs and actively showing its dislike of dogs brought to the shoot by the guns, especially guest guns who were not invited to bring their dogs.

A well-trained keeper's dog, if it is also well-trained itself, knows how to lurk under a seat in the village pub when the keeper is lurking above. Both of them, of course, are looking for the poachers and poacher's dogs.

Hounds, as all the best sporting persons know, are in a class apart and must never be referred to as 'dogs'.

Like humans who gather in packs to watch games such as tennis, cricket and football, hounds are sociable. They are, however, better disciplined and less inclined to fight among themselves than humans.

One can see hounds being sociable at Boxing Day 'meets' when people are paraded for them to see. They are especially sociable with people who have sandwiches and sausage rolls.

As well as hounds that still hunt in packs there are more aloof types of hounds. These are representatives of breeds which can no longer be hunted in Britain, anyway, because the dangerous creatures they used to hunt have all been rounded up and put into enclosures for their own safety.

Most owners of deerhounds, wolfhounds or elkhounds would be extremely surprised if they met a wolf, an elk or even a deer while going for 'last walkies' in the evening; so would many of the hounds.

Racing dogs can trace their ancestry back to the Egyptians and other ancient cultures and there is ancient graffiti to prove it. They all come from greyhound-type stock and were evolved to chase things for food for humans to eat.

Since humans have been able to obtain food from shops and supermarkets without the help of hounds, they have used some of them to obtain money by chasing furry dummies around greyhound tracks.

Others are allowed to follow their chasing instincts in open spaces and some, usually the smaller variety, are kept as pets and can provide endless fun and exercise for their owners in town and city parks.

ODD DOGS AND PET DOGS

Over the years, dog shows have been the means of introducing some exotic breeds into Western Countries. Some of them don't even look like dogs.

There are dogs with so much fur that one cannot see whether they have legs or wheels, eyes or noses. Many of them have breed names which are difficult or impossible to pronounce.

Why, one asks, is it necessary to import such weird-looking creatures when our own mongrels can do it by themselves? On the other hand, it is as well to remind ourselves, if Man had not invented breeds, we should still have only wolves on the hearth as well as at the door.

Recalling that the first plan of early dog was to obtain food and shelter without having to work too hard, it is obvious that, at the back of its mind, it had every intention of evolving into a pet animal.

There are tough dog persons such as gamekeepers, huntsmen, policemen and other professional handlers, who insist that dogs are dogs (or hounds) and should never be treated as pets.

It is odd that many of these tough dog persons seem to fail to notice that the occasional retired dog (or hound) is occupying their favourite armchair or even half their bed.

The professional sporting dogs who have cunningly made themselves pets are much resented by the representatives of breeds who consider they were intended to be pets in the first place. It is unwise to mention, in their presence, that many of them, especially those of Oriental origin, were bred to be snacks in the old days – sort of take-away Chinese hot dogs.

Since people were taken over by dogs, their homes have become pet-infested. In the good old days when good old open log fires were the source of comfort on long winter evenings, the flickering flames showed the silhouettes of little pet dogs sitting cosily in front of them.

With the increasing cost of fuel, the habit of many humans to live in flats and the introduction of central heating, modern pet dogs have had to adapt.

Comparatively few of them can sit in heaps in front of large blazing log fires these days. It is not beyond the ingenuity of small pet dogs to climb on to the top of radiators but these tend to be uncomfortable.

Nearly all small dogs, however, seem to manage to find their way into bedrooms and despite all orders not to go upstairs, go to ground in beds. Many a guest has been alarmed by a bump in the night, under the bedclothes.

Dogs must have taken advantage of vehicles drawn by horses ever since Man learned to drive horses. Big dogs like Dalmatians usually had to run behind, originally as guards but later as prestige symbols.

Small dogs, then as now, being more cunning, soon learned to cadge a lift. With the invention of the motorcar, many small dogs became bored with lying about in the back seat which was inclined to make them feel sick, anyway, and moved to the front.

If there is a small pet dog in a car, it is to be found on the passenger's seat, on the passenger or trying to drive the car.